Thy w

A sma...

FRAN GODFREY

McCrimmons
Great Wakering, Essex, England

First published in 2004 in the United Kingdom by
MCCRIMMON PUBLISHING CO. LTD.
10-12 High Street, Great Wakering, Essex SS3 0EQ
info@mccrimmons.com   www.mccrimmons.com

Text © 2004 Fran Godfrey

ISBN 0 85597 659 4

Cover image © The Benedictine Sisters of Turvey Abbey
Cover design and layout by Nick Snode
Typeset in 11/13pt Clearface Regular and 19pt Aesop
Text pages printed on Fineblade Smooth 115gsm
Cover printed on 240gsm one sided art
Printed and bound by Thanet Press Ltd., Margate, Kent.

Contents

Introduction

MY UNDERSTANDING OF PRAYER

Prayer is defined in the dictionary as 'a personal communication or petition addressed to a deity, especially in the form of supplication, adoration, praise, contrition or thanksgiving.' Put like that, it doesn't sound like a very difficult thing to do. So why is it that most of us struggle with prayer? I think one of the reasons might be that we never really *mature* in our praying.

When, as children, we were taught to pray it was very simple. Our prayers were for Mummy and Daddy and long lists of family members; for certain presents at Christmas, maybe; we then graduated to praying – pleading earnestly – for certain things to happen – or not to happen. We probably even attempted the odd bit of 'plea bargaining' – "If you let me pass this exam, I promise I'll be good for the rest of the day / week / month." As children it was hard to understand why many of our prayers seemed not to be answered – at least not in the way we thought they should be. And even as adults that same disappointment can exist. I've never forgotten a comment I read years ago from someone who observed wryly: "People who say their prayers are never answered, forget that 'No' is an answer."

It is when prayers seem to be *ignored* that some people are in serious danger of losing their faith in God, so it is vital – literally vital – that we mature in our prayers. As we get older we really do need to change – not only in the *way* we pray but also in our *attitude* to prayer.

Many people choose to pray by learning, or reading, prayers from Missals and prayer books. And, of course, in community prayer this is the only option. But when it comes to praying alone I think it is important to consider how we go about that. To return to our dictionary – one of the most telling words in the definition is the word 'personal' – 'a *personal* communication or petition'.

Imagine you invite me to come and visit you at home. I go into your sitting-room, sit down, take out a book and start reading some beautiful prose to you for ten minutes or so. Then I stand up and leave. What would you think, I wonder? Would you have learned anything at *all* about me? And yet – isn't that what we so often do when we read, or recite, prayers to God? Of course, we do need to resort to words we have learned. There have been many, many beautiful prayers composed by saintly people. And of course, Our Lord Himself taught us the most perfect prayer which we should say often and thoughtfully. But remember also in that prayer, that Our Lord taught us to call God – 'Our Father'.

It's hard to think of the Almighty God and Creator of us and everything we know as simply 'Our Father'. But that is what we have been told He wants us to do. So – imagine the most benevolent, loving person you can, your very dearest friend – and TALK to him. Tell Him about your fears, your pains, your worries, your wishes, your dreams. Be sure also to tell Him about all the things that make you happy, all the things you take for granted and shouldn't, – and THANK Him. We do have a tendency to forget (like the nine lepers) to go back and say 'thank you' when something goes right; when our prayers have been answered in the way we wanted them to be. God hears all our prayers and there are many, many times when wonderful things happen in our lives, when kindness and love are shown to us, when things turn out well – and you may be sure that God has had a hand in all of that, because those things are good – and God is goodness itself.

A word of caution: we need to be wary of turning our prayers into a litany of requests, and – sometimes, God forgive us – complaints. Personally I don't lay great store by asking for material things. My experience of praying for lottery wins proves that it doesn't work! Praying for spiritual 'things' – is different. You will get much better results if you ask for help with your hot temper, for increased faith, for endurance to suffer pain, for greater patience. And I think that God is particularly indulgent if you pray for something on behalf of someone else. I have often prayed for something as simple as fine weather on a day when I have been taking someone on an outing and poor weather would have spoiled that person's enjoyment of the day out. And invariably the weather has been good. Truly.

Constant praying – talking to God – including Him in your life and sharing everything about your life with Him, will result in the sort of closeness you achieve with your dearest friend. When God becomes the first Person you turn to in times of happiness and in times of grief, you will never be let down. You will be possessed of the strength to cope with whatever life throws at you. In sorrow and in joy you will have the most valuable gift: the inner peace and security of knowing that God is with you; that the most important thing with which to concern yourself is working towards your life with Him in heaven.

Another thought on the subject of prayer. Accept that sometimes you'll do it better than others. There are times when I can go into a church and kneel down before the Blessed Sacrament and talk to Our Lord for 20 minutes without any distraction. But not often. Usually if I spend 20 minutes on my knees I will have devoted about five of those minutes to actual prayer. The rest of the time my mind has drifted off down some alley of distraction. I don't think it matters too much. The important thing is that your *intention* is to pray, to raise heart and mind to God; that you have set aside the time to do it; that you are perhaps in a church, or on your knees or in a prayerful situation. And don't be too disheartened if you experience (as you certainly will from time to time) 'spiritual dryness' – when all attempts at prayer fail. The best we can do then is express our sorrow and disappointment and ask that we may do better next time. God made us and He knows us and all our weaknesses. And isn't it extraordinary to think that He still loves us? That thought alone should inspire us to utter prayers of humble thanksgiving and earnest supplication that we may learn to *love Him* ever more.

As you may guess, my own prayers are usually similar to my conversations with a good friend. The themes and subjects are all muddled up together as things I want to say occur to me. Of the four different types of prayer (ADORATION, CONTRITION, THANKSGIVING and PETITION) without any doubt the most important is the first, the prayer of adoration; and yet I suspect many of us work from the last through to the first – and maybe don't always reach the first. It is something we should strive to correct. The most important prayer is the one in which we recognise and acknowledge Almighty God as our Creator; the all-powerful One who holds us in our very existence. That will lead us on to feeling contrite for the many ways in which we let God down; then on to gratitude for all His endless forgiveness. Finally, we place our trust in the Lord by asking His help with the problems and worries we face daily.

Prayer has much to do with trust. Critics have said, 'What sort of God needs to be adored and told all the time that He is wonderful?' Of course, God has no need of that at all. What He desires is for us to accept our dependence on Him, acknowledge our need for Him, and demonstrate our faith in Him. All prayer shows faith. If we did not believe that God was listening, we would never bother to pray. So to pray to God is to believe in God. Faith in God ensures our ultimate salvation, which is what God wants for us and so our attempts at prayer can only be pleasing to Him.

There is a further stage to maturing in our prayers. Taking once again as the perfect reference, the prayer Our Lord gave us, it's not very long before we come across the words 'Thy will be done'. These words are easy to say, easy to forget – and the hardest to mean sincerely. We will arrive at real maturity in our spiritual lives when we can say – truly and often – 'Thy will be done.' 'Whatever you want for me, Lord, so be it. I accept absolutely and without question, your will for me, trusting that in your love and your mercy, you will never leave me to manage alone.' It's quite extraordinary how this prayer – uttered from the depth of your heart – never fails to deliver inner peace. You will find that fears are dispelled and everything falls into its right perspective. It's the acceptance within our souls that God really does know what is best for us. That can be very hard to believe sometimes when God seems to 'allow' terrible things to happen to innocent, good people. But being a follower of Christ means trusting Him, and accepting that there will be many more questions than answers. Pray to be saved from the pride which says you should understand everything; the enormous pride which says, in effect, that you think you know better than God. Remember, the words were used by Our Lord Himself in the Garden of Gethsemane (Luke 22:42) and by Our Lady at the Annunciation (Luke 1:38). We could not wish for two more compelling reasons to include the words "Thy will be done" in our daily prayers.

I know that Our Lord taught us not to 'babble' in our prayers (Matthew 6:7); but He also encouraged us to "go to your private room, shut yourself in, and so pray to your Father." (Matthew 6:6). In this little book I have tried to put together a few prayers, a few ideas suitable for your 'private room', which I hope may help to get you started on your own conversations with God, our loving Father, who longs to hear from us.

(Part of this introduction was previously reproduced in *Safe Home*, the quarterly magazine of the Little Sisters of the Poor.)

Worship/Adoration

*'Scripture says:
You must worship the Lord your God,
him alone you must serve.'*

Luke 4:8

MY LORD AND MY GOD,
how do I begin to offer you the adoration you so
    deserve?
How do I – your created one – worship you,
    my Creator?
I look around at all you have given me;
the many splendours of the beautiful world for
    me to explore;
the seasons which bring about the miraculous
    changes in nature,
as ordained by you and unassisted by man.
I see towering above me enormous trees,
and at my feet the tiniest of flowers,
the most minute, perfectly-formed creatures –
    and I marvel.
I know little of the workings of my body,
but I do know that man can create nothing as
    complex as a human being.

My brain controls the involuntary and voluntary
   actions of my organs, muscles and limbs.
Things just function and carry me through
   each day
without my having to give it a thought.
My soul forms my being with its ability to feel a
   myriad of emotions.
I cannot imagine being loved into existence
and yet I know that I have been created by you
   out of love.
And that is the most wondrous thought of all.
That thought alone brings me to my knees
   before you.
My God, I adore you
and can never cease to worship you for your
   goodness to me.

Praise

*'From the rising of the sun to its setting,
praised be the name of God.'*

Psalm 113:3

MY LORD AND MY GOD,
to recognise and fully accept
your majesty and your Godhead,
your supreme goodness and infinite power
is the start of truly praising you.
I know that I am nothing without you;
I can do nothing good without you,
I can be no one good without you.
You are my grace, my strength, my talents,
  my abilities.
You are the centre of my life and the focus of
  my day.
If you should abandon me I would be lost.
Please accept from me, your creature,
my poor attempts at offering you
all praise, all glory, all honour. Always.

Love

'Jesus said:
"If you love me you will keep my
commandments …This is my commandment:
love one another as I have loved you." '

John 14:15 and 15:12

MY LORD AND MY GOD,
I am so fortunate:
there are many people I love in many
    different ways.
I don't know why I love or how I love.
It isn't something I can be taught,
it is an ability you have given me.
There is a song which expresses the idea
    that the greatest thing in life
is to love and to be loved in return.
And I do truly believe that.
To have that closeness, that security,
that knowledge that someone cares so much
    about what happens to me
is worth more than anything in this life.
And then I must persuade myself that this is
    exactly how you love me.

Continued ☞

What can I do but love you in return?
Every day I see the hundreds of things you do to
    protect me,
to care for me, to see me over hurdles –
    and I love you.
Help me please, Lord, to know you better and
    love you more.
It can be hard to love everyone you have created,
but grant that I may never be anything but
    charitable
towards all your people, whom you love equally.

Faith

'Jesus said:
"Have faith in God…
everything you ask and pray for,
believe that you have it already,
and it will be yours." '

Mark 11:22,24

MY LORD AND MY GOD,
I thank you with all my heart for the gift of faith.
I believe in you absolutely and utterly.
The fact of your existence and your presence in
    my life
sustains me every day.
I know that your will keeps me in existence,
that your love protects me hour by hour.
And yet, you know that there is the odd day
    when doubts creep in.
It is not always easy to live as a Christian.
Those who live without faith sometimes seem to
    have an easier time.
They don't seem to have to take much
    responsibility for their deeds;

Continued ☞

they deny themselves nothing and live by a
limited set of rules.
As I struggle to live by the rules you have given
me,
I wonder sometimes – only very rarely – if I have
got it wrong.
And then I realise that if I do not have faith in
you,
I have nothing at all;
if I do not have your rules, I am rudderless;
if I do not have eternal life with you to look
forward to,
I am dead.
And most of all, I remember what you, Lord,
went through for love of me,
so that I may believe and be saved,
and I do believe.
I really do believe,
and I thank you again for that faith.

Trust

*'Jesus said,
"Do not let your hearts be troubled.
You trust in God, trust also in me." '*
John 14:1

*'When I am afraid, I put my trust in you,
in God, whose word I praise,
in God I put my trust and have no fear,
what power has human strength over me?'*
Psalm 56:3

MY LORD AND MY GOD,
I trust in you.
I trust in your endless mercy,
your boundless love,
your infinite goodness,
your patience with me when I fail you.
Whatever happens to me in this life
I trust that your love
means that you will never leave me to manage
    alone.
You are always beside me and within me.
Whatever pains I may suffer,
nothing and no one can ever truly hurt me.
You are with me – all is well.

Continued ☞

I accept utterly, Lord,
that in all things
your will, not mine, must be done.

Hope

*'Be brave, take heart,
all who put your hope in God.'*

Psalm 31:24

*'Rest in God alone, my soul!
He is the source of my hope.'*

Psalm 62:5

MY LORD AND MY GOD,
I have done much in my life which has
    been displeasing to you.
I know that Jesus your Son
came to earth as Man and suffered an
    agonising death
to atone for the sins of us all.
Because of your immense love
I dare to hope that one day
you will allow me to be united with you,
see you face to face
in your glorious kingdom,
where there will be no further temptations,
no more pain,
no more fear
no more weeping.

Continued ☞

In this I hope;
for that day I long.
Help me to do everything in this life
that will bring me closer to you in the next.

Contrítion

*'I acknowledge my guilt
and grieve over my sin.'*

Psalm 38:19

MY LORD AND MY GOD,
how do I ever say sorry for all the ways in which
    I have offended you?
I struggle daily to fight temptation,
to draw away from the magnetic pull of my
    fallen nature.
And I fail, again and again.
I hide my face in shame before you.
And then I remind myself of your love for me,
and I dare to look up and beg forgiveness
    once more.
I acknowledge absolutely my wrong-doing;
it is no one's fault but mine that I have
    sinned again.
Sometimes when I manage, by your grace, to
    avoid major sins,
I think things are going a little better,
and then I realise how many flaws there are in
    my character:

Continued ☞

my intolerance, impatience, self-importance,
    jealousy –
the list is endless –
and I realise how very far I have to go before
I can be perfect as my 'Father in heaven
    is perfect'.
I know I cannot attain this perfection
until I am allowed to be with you in heaven.
Help me please to keep on trying.
I know that there is no sin I can commit
which is outside your capacity for forgiveness
as long as I am truly contrite.
Help me to see myself as you see me;
to see my faults honestly
and work to correct them one by one.
My Lord, I need you.

Sorrow/Grief

'Many are the sorrows of the wicked,
but love surrounds those
who trust in the Lord.'

Psalm 32:10

MY LORD AND MY GOD,
sometimes it seems that there are so many
   things around me
which cause me sorrow and grief:
the wrongs we do to each other,
the loss we feel when we lose a loved one,
the burdens of worry for our family,
the increasing concerns of advancing age,
the weaknesses of a frail body,
the succumbing to temptation.
All these things seem to pile on to my shoulders
   and weigh me down.
Sometimes I feel that I really cannot manage
   any more.
At times like these I turn to thoughts of you;
of your grief at what you see your people do to
   one another;
what you suffered to try and show the world
   what is right,   Continued ☞

what we need to do to be saved,
and your sorrow at the world's constant rejection
    of you.
And I think of how much you care for me,
how you are always there, ready to shoulder
    the burdens with me.
As long as I keep my eyes and my heart fixed
    on you
even though no one else may be around,
I know I am not alone; you are always with me.
One day, if it is your will, I will know only tears
    of joy.

Joy

*'Jesus said, "Until now you have not asked
anything in my name.
Ask and you will receive,
and so your joy will be complete." '*

John 16:24

*'My lips sing for joy...
because you have redeemed me.'*

Psalm 71:23

MY LORD AND MY GOD,
today I feel happy and at peace.
The world around me is full of good things and
  kind people.
My heart is singing, all is going so well.
How can I thank you for all the good things
  around me?
I know it is your doing.
I know that you care for me and that you are
  smiling on me.
I can only think happy thoughts today.
I contemplate your goodness,
I treasure all you have given me –
my home, my friends, my family, my health.

Continued ☞

I treasure most of all my faith in you,
your presence in my heart and in my life.
I treasure the promise you have made that
    I will be with you one day.
Perhaps tomorrow things may look less rosy,
but I know that I will never lose your love for me.
That is always there – on the stormy days and
    on the sunny days.
And that is something to make me rejoice always.
May I never forget to turn to you in these times
    of joy
as well as in times of sorrow.

Thanks

*'Give thanks to God for he is good,
his faithful love lasts for ever.'*

Psalm 107:1

MY LORD AND MY GOD,
it is too easy to find things in life about which
    to complain.
Of course every life has its problems,
every human being suffers some pain
    at some time.
May I never become so blinded by complaints
that I fail to see the good around me.
Remind me, when things go wrong,
to look at what has gone right.
Help me to be grateful for the wonderful things
    in my life.
However bleak things may be sometimes,
let me recognise the brightness which is
    always there –
even if it is in the distance.
All sadness passes as surely as day follows night.
I thank you with all of my heart and all
    of my soul
for the love you have shown me, Continued ☞

the good things you have given me,
the security of my faith in your mercy and care.
I know you will never leave me as long as I keep
    turning to you,
and for that I can never say 'thank you' enough.
May I never forget to be thankful
for all the good things which are too numerous
    to count.
My God, I love you.

In times of sickness or pain

'Jesus said:
"In all truth I tell you,
you will be weeping and wailing
while the world will rejoice;
you will be sorrowful,
but your sorrow will turn to joy." '

John 16:20

MY LORD AND MY GOD,
how hard life can seem when we are plagued
  with illness or pain.
It is difficult to think of anything else
when discomfort, distress, or even agony crowds
  in on us
and we are reminded of how very frail our
  human condition can be.
Help me at those times to remember
that you have suffered much more than I am
  being asked to bear,
and as well you bore great indignity and scorn on
  my behalf.

Continued ☞

Help me to unite my small sufferings to yours
and offer them in some small penance for my
  many sins against you.
You are the physician who can heal me;
your care and love can lighten my burdens
  and ease my pains.
As I turn to you and accept your will for me
I feel an easing of my suffering
and a closeness to you which no human ailment
  can spoil.
I know that my body is just a shell,
and that if I can keep a healthy soul, I shall
  be saved.
Stay with me, my Lord, and all is well.

At times of worry or fear

'Jesus said,
"Every hair on your head has been counted.
So there is no need to be afraid;" '

Matthew 10:30

MY LORD AND MY GOD,
there are times when my worries overwhelm me.
I feel alone with my fears, and panic grips me.
Nobody can really understand how I am
    feeling inside
and the loneliness of that is terrifying.
It is at times like these that I rush to you.
Please console me and give me the strength
to see things in their right perspective.
Nothing in this world is that important.
All that matters is the knowledge
that you know and understand.
Calm my fears,
ease my mind,
steady my heart.
With you I can manage everything.
Let me always feel your presence within me
as you pour your love over my troubled soul.
In all things, Lord, let your will be done.

For wisdom

*'The beginning of wisdom
is the fear of the LORD,
and knowledge of the Holy One
is understanding.'*

Proverbs 9:10

MY LORD AND MY GOD,
I have thought about this
and I know that you are a loving and merciful God.
I don't think you want me to be frightened of you;
what you want –
the very least of what is owing to you –
is my respect
and my understanding that at the end of time
I will face you with all the actions of my life
laid out before me
for you to scrutinize and judge.
I know that I must face your judgement
and I know your justice can only be perfect.
I pray now for the wisdom to see always your will
    for me,
and for the strength to obey you,
to serve you as you wish,
to be the person you created me to be.

Send me the Holy Spirit, I pray,
so that any judgements and decisions
    I must make
may be absolutely fair, merciful
and touched with your wisdom.

For peace

Jesus said,
"Peace I bequeath to you,
my own peace I give you,
a peace which the world cannot give,
this is my gift to you.
Do not let your hearts be troubled or afraid."

John 14:27

MY LORD AND MY GOD,
if only everyone in your world could take your peace
    into their hearts.
Knowledge and understanding of your love
    brings your peace.
It's a depth of peace
which can come from nothing in this world.
It is a feeling deep within the soul
that nothing in this life can hurt us
in any way that is important.
Grant that I may feel this peace, this serenity,
    always.
I pray that everyone may seek this sort of peace;
a fair and tolerant attitude towards our neighbour;
an acceptance of our differences;
respect and consideration for all.

In other words, Lord,
may we all love one another as you commanded,
    as you love us.

For loved ones

*'Love is always patient and kind;
love is never jealous;
love is not boastful or conceited,
it is never rude… it does not take offence or
store up grievances.
Love does not rejoice at wrongdoing,
but finds its joy in the truth.
It is always ready to make allowances,
to trust to hope
and to endure whatever comes.'*

1 Corinthians 13:4–7

MY LORD AND MY GOD,
I am much blessed:
there are people I love
and I know I am loved too.
And yet I read what St Paul wrote about love
and what is required of me,
ad I know that I fall well short of perfect love.
However much I love someone
I do lose my patience sometimes,
I snap unkindly,
I forget to be attentive,
I act selfishly or jealously.

I pray that I may imitate your love for me
with your endless patience, compassion
    and understanding.
I pray that those I love
may be spared worry, illness and distress of
    any sort.
I pray most of all that you will be with us at
    all times,
guiding us, protecting us
and reminding us how to love one another
    unconditionally
as you love us.

On bereavement

'Jesus said:
"Anyone who believes in me,
even though that person dies, will live,
and whoever lives and believes in me
will never die." '

John 11:25–26

MY LORD AND MY GOD,
my heart is lead within me,
my eyes are burning with tears,
and my mind so full of my loved one who has
    gone from me
that I am barely able to think of anything else.
I feel there is a chasm in my life which can never
    be filled;
an ache in my heart which can never be healed.
And then Lord I remember your love for me,
and your promise that he who believes will
    never die.
As surely as you created each of us,
so you take each one back to be with you.
Forgive my selfishness
in wanting to hold on to those I love;

I know and I trust that they will soon be home
    with you,
in perfect peace and absolute happiness;
with no more pain or tears.
Grant eternal rest to them and to all the holy
    souls, Almighty God;
grant that I, too, may join you
when it is time for you to call me to your
    holy Kingdom
when all tears will be wiped away.
With you, my Lord, I can smile again.

Before Holy Mass

'Jesus said:
"This is my body given for you;
do this in remembrance of me." '

Luke 22:19

MY LORD AND MY GOD,
help me to prepare to celebrate this Holy Mass
    devoutly and reverently.
I have attended Mass many times,
and sometimes it is easy to let the prayers and
    actions of the priest wash over me
and bypass me
as my mind wanders off in other directions.
May I never forget the immense sacrifice
    you offered
when you died in redemption of my sins.
May I remember that, every time I go to Mass,
I am trying to share with you
    your Last Supper;
    the days of your suffering,
    death and resurrection,
May I feel with you your pain,
    your disappointment,
    your dejection

and your ultimate joy as you achieved
    your Father's will.
I offer myself,
my heart, soul and mind
    for you to fill.
Be with me as surely as you are here
    present on the altar.
I prostrate myself before you.

After Holy Mass

MY LORD AND MY GOD,
I thank you with all my heart, my soul and
   my understanding
for the graces and the blessings of this
   Holy Mass.
I thank you for the immeasurable gift of
   your Body
given to feed my soul and my heart;
I thank you for the gift of your life,
given to save my wretched, sin-filled life.
Stay with me now
as surely as I have received your sacred Body
in the Blessed Sacrament.
Fill me with your grace and your strength,
possess me utterly,
flood me with your goodness,
so that everything I think, do and say
may come from you
and return to give you greater glory.

Before confession

'Peter said,
"Lord, how often must I forgive my brother
if he wrongs me? As often as seven times?"
Jesus answered,
"Not seven, I tell you,
but seventy-seven times." '

Matthew 18:21–22

MY LORD AND MY GOD,
where do I start?
I long to make a good Confession.
Help me to examine my conscience with honesty
    and clarity.
Let me remember all my wrongs against you and
    my neighbour.
It can be easy to try and make excuses
    sometimes
for things which turned out badly,
when I have acted less than charitably.
I know that I can hide nothing from you,
and that you see through all excuses.
Help me to see myself as you see me,
so that I may identify more honestly my faults
and work hard to erase them.

Continued ☞

I trust in your endless mercy and compassion
that you will forgive me yet again,
and will grant me the strength to persevere
carrying the cross of my sinful human nature
    with me.
I know that your repeated forgiveness lightens
    its load.

After confession

'Jesus said,
"Whose sins you forgive,
they are forgiven." '

John 20:23

MY LORD AND MY GOD,
It seems that every time I come to
 the confessional
I am repeating the same sins over and
 over again.
I am ashamed that I don't seem to be getting
 any better.
Help me to change;
I need your grace to transform me
into the person I long to be – for love of you.
I thank you with all my heart
for the graces I have received from your
sacrament of reconciliation.
I feel a joy and lightness in my soul
that I am – at least for now – free of sin;
that my soul has been washed clean
 by your grace.
I can go out into the world with a
 clear conscience,

Continued ☞

ready to start afresh, ready to love my neighbour,
determined not to fall again.
Grant me your strength and I can succeed.

To the Holy Spirit

'Jesus said:
"If you then, evil as you are,
know how to give your children what is good,
how much more will the heavenly Father
give the Holy Spirit to those who ask him!"'

Luke 11:13

MY LORD AND MY GOD,
I pray that you may enable me to open my heart
to receive your Holy Spirit.
Blessed Spirit of God,
come to me,
fill me with your grace, your strength, your truth.
Grant me your wisdom so that I may choose wisely;
your compassion, so that I may treat everyone
   with kindness;
your fortitude so that I may bear without
   complaint
every hardship which may come my way;
your vision so that I may see the Father's will
   for me;
your strength so that I may obey;
your generosity so that I may give without
   counting the cost.

Continued ☞

You are my conscience,
my talent, the life in my soul.
You are the goodness in me,
I beseech you never to abandon me, or I am lost.

To Our Lady

Mary said,
"Behold, I am the handmaid of the Lord.
May it be done to me
according to your word."

Luke 1:38

MARY, QUEEN AND MOTHER,
you gave us the perfect example of how to respond
    to the will of God.
Without thought for yourself,
you accepted everything that was to come in
    your life.
Please intercede for us;
pray for us
that we may be moved to follow your example
and to listen to God's word
through your beloved Son, Jesus Christ.
You showed us the way
by fixing your sights always on Jesus,
by storing His words in your heart,
by accompanying Him through His sufferings
and by standing bravely at the foot of the cross
where He died for us.

Continued ☞

You witnessed your beloved Son's bitter sufferings
when you were powerless to protect Him,
and yet your faith was such
that your trust in Almighty God never wavered.
Imprint on my soul
your humility, your patience,
your kindness and your purity;
may I find true inspiration in your example
    of perfection
and one day be with you and your beloved Son
in the glorious kingdom of heaven.

To Saint Peter

'Jesus said:
"I say to you: you are Peter
and on this rock I will build my church.
…I will give you the keys
of the kingdom of Heaven:
whatever you bind on earth
will be bound in heaven;
whatever you loose on earth
will be loosed in heaven." '

Matthew 16:18–19

DEAR SAINT PETER,
whenever I read of you in the gospels
my heart is filled with deepest affection, respect
   and gratitude.
I love your enthusiasm,
your impulsiveness,
your absolute love for Jesus,
your great desire to protect Him and save Him
from the death He had to endure.
I understand and can readily identify with
   your fear
when it forced you to deny your friendship
   with Jesus.

Continued ☞

I feel for you in your abject sorrow
   and desolation
and your utter penitence as you wept for what
   you had done.
And most of all
I draw great consolation from Our Lord's ready
   forgiveness
when he saw your sorrow.
You went on to die for love of Christ
and for what you knew to be true.
I ask that you may pray for us here,
as we struggle with faith and life,
grateful for your leadership of the infant Church
   on earth.
Please also pray for our present Pope
that he may continue in your footsteps,
   guiding Christ's Church
with the wisdom and strength of the Holy Spirit.
Saint Peter – pray for us.

Morning prayer

*'Each morning fill us with your faithful love,
we shall sing and be happy all our days.'*

Psalm 90:14

MY LORD AND MY GOD,
I thank you for my rest
and for bringing me safely through the night.
I pray that you may continue to guard me and
    guide me
through this new day.
Grant that I may see your will for me, and obey it;
that I may treat with kindness and respect
    everyone I meet,
that I may perform every action with charity in
    my heart,
that I may offer my whole day to you.
Use me, Lord, as you will;
I am your servant and I love you.

Night prayer

'On my bed when I think of you,
I muse on you in the watches of the night;
for you have always been my help;
in the shadow of your wings I rejoice;
my heart clings to you,
your right hand supports me.'

Psalm 63:6–8

MY LORD AND MY GOD,
the day is over and I am weary.
I offer you my grateful thanks
for the graces and blessings of this day;
for your loving guidance
in helping me over the hurdles,
for your hand in the good things which
    have happened.
For your consolation when things went not so well.
I beg your forgiveness
for all the ways in which I have caused you
pain or disappointment.
Send your angels to watch over us this night.
grant me and those I love and care for
a peaceful and restful night's sleep.

If it is your will, Lord, bring us, safely to
    a new day
and grant that then we may serve you better,
love you more deeply and draw ever closer to you.

Thy will be done

"Our Father in heaven,
may your name be held holy,
your kingdom come,
your will be done, on earth as in heaven."

Matthew 6:9–10

MY LORD AND MY GOD,
whatever sun shines in my life,
whatever storms rage,
whatever joys come my way,
whatever sufferings I am asked to endure,
whatever problems cause me concern,
whatever insults are heaped on me,
whatever love is shown to me,
whatever thou asks of me,
in all things and at all times,
may I always say and truly mean –
thy will be done.

Amen

When it is hard to pray

FINALLY, I have included the following meditation that I wrote a few years ago at the request of an elderly lady. She was living in a residential care home, was bed-ridden and very frail. She said she had lost the ability to pray; her ability to concentrate was much reduced. I reproduce this here in case it might be of help to others. I know that dear Heather, may God have mercy on her soul, would have wanted me to.

When "the spirit is willing,
but the flesh is weak"

Matthew 26:41

"Come to me all you ... who are
overburdened and I will give you rest."

Matthew 11:28

LORD, MY GOD,
I can't really say that I am overburdened,
nor that I need to be granted rest.
I have all the physical rest I want.
No one makes any demands on me.
To be honest, I wish I didn't have to have so
  much rest.

Continued ☞

I wish I had some strength
to be active in some small way.
But then, maybe Lord,
it is you who has given me this rest.
With my body incapable of activity,
it has become my burden.
And so I bring myself and my burden to you.
Where my strength has failed
let me lean on you.
You know all things, Lord,
you know what I feel,
where it hurts,
how frustrated I can become.
Make me a good patient.
Help me to accept the goodness of others
when it is offered.
Keep me from complaining;
I know I can never endure
what you endured without complaint,
but help me to be just a bit more like you.

*"I am the light of the world; anyone who
follows me ... will have the light of life."*

John 8:12

MY LORD,
With so much time on my hands
praying should be easy.
I have so few decisions to make,
no problems to solve,
really nothing to absorb my attention.
I should be able to turn my thoughts
towards you.
And yet my mind is vacant;
my thoughts seem to be of nothing.
I want to be able
to thank you for so much.
My life has been filled with many good things.
It has been enriched by many kind friends.
I have found much to make me laugh
and much to make me cry.
I thank you for the ability to feel emotion.
Without the sadness in my life,
I could never have appreciated the happiness,
in the same way that I could not know
what it is to be in the light,
if I had never experienced darkness.

Continued ☞

Remind me, Lord, of the wonderful things
   in my life.
Help me to see the good things
which are yet around me.
I still have much to be thankful for.
Let me continue to see the light –
and know that it comes from you.

> *"Do not let your hearts be troubled.*
> *Trust in God, trust also in me."*
>
> John 14:1

LORD, MY GOD,
I do trust in you.
Absolutely and utterly.
It is one of the few strengths remaining in me.
And I thank you for it.
Am I being complacent?
I know that there is much in me
that needs to be forgiven.
It's easy to think that
when we reach old age and infirmity,
it's impossible to sin.
But that is mistaken thinking.
Clear my mind, Lord,

and help me to see where and how
I still go wrong, still cause you offence.
Am I impatient or bad-tempered?
Am I less than charitable in word and deed?
Am I as grateful as I should be?
I need your guidance, my Lord.
I need you to sharpen my conscience.
Show me my faults here and now,
not when I come face to face with you
as I so long to do.
Keep me steadfast in loving you
and serving you in whatever way I can.
Grant me the patience to accept your will for me.
And may my journey to your side
be easy and pain-free.
In all things, my Lord and my God,
let your will be done.